HERITAGE
of Ireland

PETER ZÖLLER

D1402594

Gill & Macmillan

Gill & Macmillan Ltd
Hume Avenue, Park West, Dublin 12
with associated companies throughout the world
www.gillmacmillan.ie
Photographs © Peter Zöller 2001
Text © Gill & Macmillan 2001
0 7171 3157 2
Design and Repro by Ultragraphics, Dublin
Map by EastWest Mapping
Printed in Spain

The paper used in this book comes from the wood pulp of managed forests. For every tree felled, at least one tree is planted, thereby renewing natural resources.

A CIP catalogue record for this book is available from the British Library.

5 4 3 2 1

Introduction

Heritage is one of those words that can mean everything and nothing. It is widely used in tourism simply to mean 'history' or 'the past'. Perhaps 'inheritance' or 'legacy' is nearer the mark. One dictionary definition gets even closer: 'anything transmitted from ancestors or past ages'. This collection of photographs by Peter Zöller is concerned with precisely that sense of what has been transmitted from the past.

The island of Ireland has been inhabited continuously since the end of the Ice Age. In common with all of north-west Europe, the proximity of the Gulf Stream means that the climate is much milder than one would expect so far north. Look at the rest of the northern hemisphere: fertile, mild Ireland is on the same parallel with bleak, frozen Labrador and with much of Siberia. In the southern hemisphere, you have to go down to Tierra del Fuego or the Falkland Islands to be as far from the equator as Ireland. Even the southern tip of New Zealand – which we think of as being very far away – is as near to the equator as the centre of France.

Ireland is a friendly space. From the dawn of history, it has been possible to settle here, to raise families, to cultivate land and livestock, to build and to bequeath. And so successive waves of settlers, invaders, plunderers and adventurers have come to Ireland. All have left their mark. From the Stone-Age fields and walls buried beneath the blanket bog of the Ceide Fields in north Mayo to the latest high-tech architecture, the island bears the imprint of human settlement.

This does not just mean buildings. Newgrange and the Rock of Cashel may be among the most dramatic and visible evidence of human achievement in Ireland but they are not the whole picture. The very landscape itself – often so deceptively timeless in appearance – has been profoundly moulded to human requirements.

As we look along a fertile river valley or across the rolling acres of the Golden Vale, it is hard to realise that for much of recorded history this was all dense deciduous woodland. Much of the island was wooded until a few hundred years ago. Towns and cities are basically the product of the last thousand years. But Ireland has been inhabited for ten thousand years. Most of what we can see today has in fact obliterated the earlier nine millennia of human settlement. Newgrange or the Poulnabrone Dolmen or the Ceide Fields are wonderful precisely because they are the exceptions to the general rule.

It is all too easy to say simply that Ireland has had a troubled past. Of course it has had in some senses. But so have most countries. Ireland never saw fighting as vicious, prolonged or socially destructive as the Thirty Years War in Germany. Ireland's religious quarrels are not unique in Europe or the rest of the world. No conflict even remotely as catastrophic as the American Civil War ever happened here. Ireland has had her troubles – most notably the awful trauma of the Great Famine (1845-52) – but looking at these photographs it is the continuities that strike the viewer, not a sense of dislocation.

Those continuities do not mean an absence of change. On the contrary, the island has been transformed many times. As we saw, the woodlands have only been cleared in the last few centuries. The small fields enclosed by their endless webs of hedgerows, which seem so emblematic of the country, are even more recent. The traditional Irish pub is generally no more than a hundred years old. Settlements have grown to villages, villages to towns, and towns to cities. Most of what visitors come to see in Dublin dates only from the eighteenth century, but the city has existed in some shape or form for more than a thousand years.

No: the continuity has to do with the steady accumulation of human achievement in town and country over many generations. Behind everything we see in Ireland – behind these photographs – that is the bottom line.

There have of course been destructive episodes – the dissolution of the many fine abbeys and monasteries by Henry VIII was a particularly savage blow, robbing the country of an irreplaceable network of superb buildings – but they have always been followed by renewal, rebuilding, replanting and new harvests. The Famine left a terrible legacy of demoralisation and emigration. But even in this instance it sparked a determination that such a catastrophe should never happen again. That determination was the motor force behind the Irish political revolution that led to the break with Britain and the creation of the Republic of Ireland.

The country has never been richer than now. The sudden spurt in Ireland's material fortunes, driven by the famous Celtic Tiger, has seen levels of personal wealth in the Republic approach the norm for the European Union. Of course, this conceals large pockets of remaining poverty but is at least a move in the right direction. In Northern Ireland, the nervous peace that has brought an apparent end to the Troubles has been another source of optimism. We hold our breath, but we hold it in hope.

These wonderful photographs are a cross-section, a kaleidoscope of human achievement in the island of Ireland across the ages. They mark the hand of man upon the land. **Heritage of Ireland** *is a photographic record and memory of the many millennia of human life on this small island.*

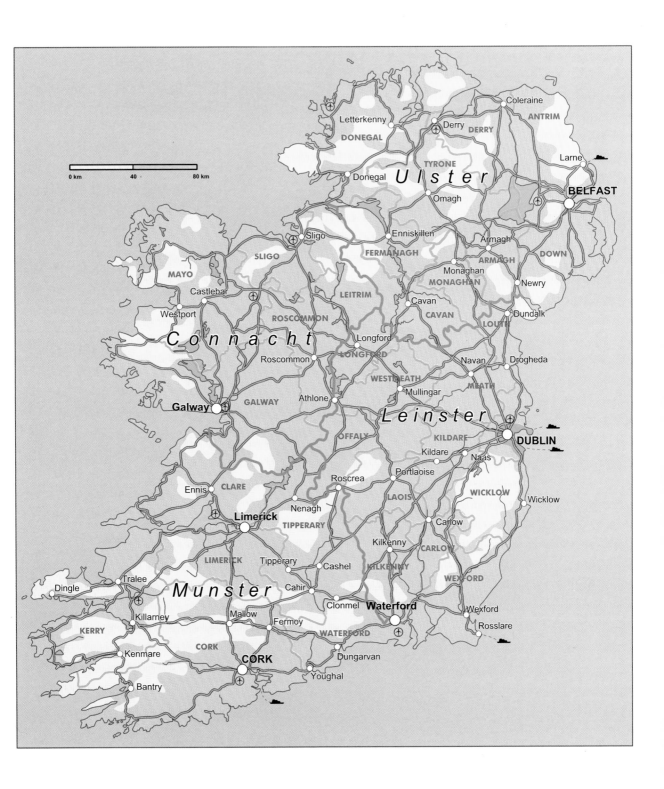

The Old Library in Trinity College dates from the early eighteenth century, although the great barrel-vaulted ceiling is a nineteenth-century addition. The Book of Kells is housed in this building. The original architect was Thomas Burgh.

The sea is never far away in Dublin, although one can often be unaware of it in the city centre. However, Dublin wraps itself around its bay like a large letter C. The view from Dalkey Hill (below) looks north across the bay towards the city centre. At the northern end of the bay stands the village of Howth (below left) with its harbour and the little island of Ireland's Eye a short distance off shore. Further north along the coast, the pretty fishing village of Skerries (left) is within easy commuting distance of the city.

Doheny & Nesbitt's pub in Lower Baggot Street (above) is deservedly one of the most famous of Dublin's traditional pubs. As it states on the awning it was established in 1867, barely twenty years after the horrific Great Famine that is remembered in the Famine memorial sculptures by Rowan Gillespie (right) which stand on Custom House Quay opposite the International Financial Services Centre. By way of total contrast, the State Apartments in Dublin Castle (below) convey a sense of classical luxury and order.

The Irish Film Centre in Temple Bar (above) shows how an intelligent restoration of old Dublin can create a vibrant modern space. The calm symmetry of classical Dublin is seen in the Georgian town houses on the Grand Canal at Mespil Road (above right) and in the fine doorway of number 38 Merrion Square (far right). A different kind of harmony and order in St Stephen's Green, the city's favourite public park (right).

Dublin is divided by the River Liffey (above)
seen here flowing under the Halfpenny Bridge.
The city first developed on the hill just south of the
river where Christ Church cathedral (below) now
stands. Grafton Street (left) is the city's most
fashionable shopping street.

The area known as the Liberties lies just to the
west of St Patrick's cathedral. The photograph
(right) shows the street memorial erected in 1929
to commemorate the centenary of Catholic
Emancipation. It stands at the junction of
Reginald Street and Gray Street just off the
Coombe.

King John's Castle in Carlingford, Co. Louth, with Slieve Foye behind.

Louth is the smallest county in Ireland but it contains many interesting antiquities. The octagonal lavabo at the Cistercian monastery of Mellifont (left) is among them. Mellifont was destroyed at the dissolution of the monasteries in 1539. The pretty garden in Carlingford (above) stands in front of the Holy Trinity interpretative centre. One of Drogheda's old town gates (right) still survives, having witnessed much of the town's turbulent history.

Co. Meath, just to the north-west of Dublin, is flat, rich, rolling countryside. The principal river is the Boyne, seen (below) flowing past Trim Castle, one of the largest Norman fortifications in Ireland. Nearby, the remains of the old Columban monastery at Kells are marked by the round tower and the high cross (above left). Most dramatic of all is Newgrange (above right), a Neolithic burial site as old as the Egyptian pyramids. It has now been completely excavated and is one of the most spectacular sights in Ireland.

Co. Kildare, immediately to the south-west of Dublin, is flat and fertile. This was the heartland of the great FitzGerald dynasty in medieval times. In the eighteenth century, two of Ireland's finest classical houses, Carton and Castletown (above right, Slidefile) were built here. Castletown dates from the 1720s and is the most imposing country house in Ireland. The Grand Canal, seen (above, Slidefile) at Robertstown, connected Dublin to the Shannon. The Japanese Gardens near Kildare town (below right, Slidefile) were laid out in the early years of the twentieth century and are a popular attraction for visitors.

*Co. Wicklow contrasts. Pleasant countryside beside Blessington Lakes (above)
and the wilder hill landscape near the Sally Gap (below).*

Wicklow is a county of varied landscapes ranging from a coastal plain to beautiful, desolate uplands. The valley of Glendalough, in the centre of the county, contains the impressive remains of the monastic settlement originally established there by St Kevin in the sixth century, including the later round tower (left). Russborough House (above), near Blessington in the west of the county, was originally built for a wealthy brewer and is one of the most impressive classical country houses in Ireland. The terraces at Powerscourt, near Enniskerry (above left) are a particularly fine example of Victorian garden design.

Co. Leitrim is dominated by the River Shannon (below) which effectively divides it in two. The county town is Carrick-on-Shannon (left). In common with other under-developed parts of Ireland, a narrow-gauge railway was built here in the late nineteenth century. Never a commercial success, the Cavan & Leitrim has long since closed for business. But happily, a section of the line has been re-opened for leisure travellers, based at the station in Dromod, Co. Leitrim (above).

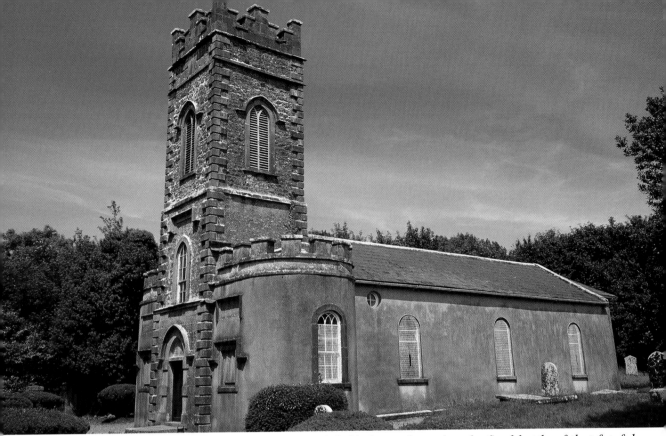

The 1798 memorial at Ballinamuck, Co. Longford (left). It was here that the final battle of that fateful year was fought, as the English under Lord Cornwallis defeated a small French invasion force. A later revolutionary was Sean MacEoin, one of the leading figures of the War of Independence (1919-21), who was known as the Blacksmith of Ballinalee and is commemorated appropriately outside his old forge (below). Longford was also the home county of the writer Oliver Goldsmith (1728-74), whose father was rector of Forgney church (above), near Ballymahon.

The ruins of Boyle Abbey, Co. Roscommon (left), probably the most impressive Cistercian abbey in Ireland. Above are some of its outbuildings. The great house at Strokestown, Co. Roscommon (below) was designed by the famous eighteenth-century architect, Richard Castle. It was the ancestral home of the Mahon family, but in recent years the stables have been turned into a very impressive Famine museum.

Athlone Castle, Co. Westmeath (left) dominated the most strategic crossing point on the middle reaches of the River Shannon. As such it ensured the growth of the surrounding town which developed on both sides of the river, but principally on the eastern bank in Co. Westmeath. This midland county is a mixture of good farmland and a number of very beautiful lakes. The monastic ruins of Fore (below left) recall an old Benedictine foundation while the premises of Locke's Distillery in Kilbeggan (below) is a picturesque reminder of a more secular activity.

The weir on the River Shannon at Athlone with the cathedral in the background.

Co. Cavan is the most southerly of the nine Ulster counties and is criss-crossed with a series of rivers and lakes. Ballyhaise House (above, Slidefile) is an impressive nineteenth-century neo-classical house in the north of the county, while further south, the pretty town of Virginia – named for Queen Elizabeth I of England – stands on the shores of Lough Ramor (below, Slidefile).

Two musicians outside a pub in Banagher, Co. Offaly (above). By far the most significant antiquity in this midland county is the great monastic centre of Clonmacnoise (left and far left) which stands on the banks of the Shannon. Originally founded in 549 by St Ciaran, it established an international reputation in medieval times as a centre of scholarship. It survived many depredations by raiders of every kind until finally plundered by the English garrison from Athlone in 1552. None the less, it is one of the most impressive sites in all Ireland.

Birr Castle, Co. Offaly (below), is the home of the earls of Rosse. The 3rd earl (1800-1867) was an astronomer and the constructor of what was then the largest telescope in the world (above) which still stands in the castle grounds.

The Rock of Dunamase, near Portlaoise, Co. Laois, is an ancient fortification. It occupies a site that dominates the flat surrounding countryside.

The pretty estate town of Abbeyleix, on the N8, was originally developed by the de Vesci family, the local landlords. It is a model estate town, as can be seen from the charming cottages (below) built with care and maintained with pride. On the main street, Morrissey's (above) is one of the best-loved pubs in the whole country. It refused to modernise when that was all the rage and now fashion has come full circle. This is arguably the most unspoiled traditional public house in Ireland. Emo Court (above right) is one of the best classical houses in the midlands. Another regional treat is the annual Stradbally steam rally (right), which attracts enthusiasts from far and wide.

Leighlinbridge, Co. Carlow, the first bridge ever built across the River Barrow.
The 'Black Castle' was built beside it to guard this vital crossing.

Co. Carlow, in the fertile south-east of the country, is drained by the Barrow, the second longest river in Ireland. The eighteenth-century navigation system (above) enabled barges to penetrate up-river into the heart of the Irish midlands. Bagenalstown (left) is also on the river just a few miles south of Leighlinbridge (below).

Kilkenny is one of the most historic counties in Ireland. Its great cathedral of St Canice (left) dates from the late thirteenth century. It was heavily restored in the nineteenth century and is beautifully maintained. The imposing Kilkenny Castle (above), was started in the early thirteenth century, although much of the present structure dates from reconstructions in the seventeenth and nineteenth centuries. The beautiful village of Inistioge (below), south of the city on the River Nore, is typical of this lovely inland county.

The Marble City Bar (left) is one of the most famous pubs in Kilkenny. The pretty town of Thomastown (below) is in the south of the county. Although the Nore is the river most associated with Co. Kilkenny, the Barrow runs along its eastern boundary and is seen (right) at Graiguenamanagh with its fine eighteenth-century bridge, and again in the tranquil view below right.

Two very different towers in Co. Waterford. The great round tower at Ardmore (above) and Reginald's Tower (right), in the city, all that remains of Waterford's Viking fortifications.

Lismore Castle, Co. Waterford, Irish home of the dukes of Devonshire.

A fine pub front in Dungarvan, Co. Waterford (above) and a view of Waterford city from the River Suir (below) showing Reginald's Tower in the left foreground. In medieval times Waterford was the most important city in Ireland after Dublin.

The town of Wexford, at the mouth of the River Slaney, with its distinctive modern bridge.

Co. Wexford, at the south-east corner of Ireland, was the centre of the 1798 rising. The principal battle of the rebellion was fought on the streets of New Ross (opposite above) which stands near the mouth of the River Barrow. Nearby, the ruins of Dunbrody Abbey (above), a Cistercian foundation, lie in pleasant countryside. Enniscorthy (below), in the centre of the county, is dominated by its sixteenth-century castle, which now houses the county museum. The final battle of the 1798 rising was fought at Vinegar Hill just outside the town. The pretty seaside village of Kilmore Quay (opposite below) is a popular summer venue for holidaymakers.

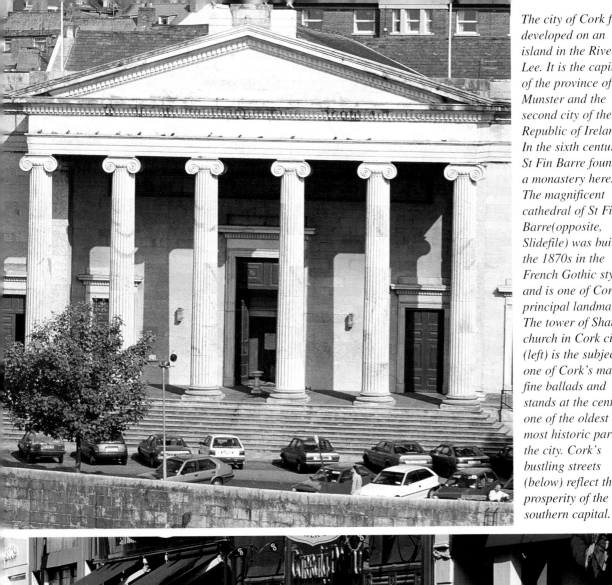

The city of Cork first developed on an island in the River Lee. It is the capital of the province of Munster and the second city of the Republic of Ireland. In the sixth century, St Fin Barre founded a monastery here. The magnificent cathedral of St Fin Barre(opposite, Slidefile) was built in the 1870s in the French Gothic style and is one of Cork's principal landmarks. The tower of Shandon church in Cork city (left) is the subject of one of Cork's many fine ballads and stands at the centre of one of the oldest and most historic parts of the city. Cork's bustling streets (below) reflect the prosperity of the southern capital.

St Patrick's Hill in Cork city (left, Slidefile).
The great harbour of Cork at dusk, with the town of Cobh and its magnificent cathedral and waterfront in the distance (above).
Roches Point at the outer limits of Cork harbour (below). The harbour, which runs first up to Cobh and then up the River Lee to the city itself, is the finest deep water berthage in the south of Ireland. The Titanic sailed pass this point on its fatal maiden voyage in 1912.

Cork city and county contain some of the most dramatically varied scenery in Ireland. The historic town of Youghal (opposite above) was home to Sir Walter Raleigh in the sixteenth century. Its distinctive clock tower (opposite bottom right) was built in 1777 and served as the town jail for a while. Bantry House (above) stands at the head of the magnificent Bantry Bay with ravishing views between the mountains and the sea. The parish church of Castletownsend (opposite bottom left) will forever be associated with the writings of Edith Somerville. Also in west Cork, the wild and dramatic scenery around Glengarriff (below) is typical of the rugged Atlantic coastal area.

Kinsale (above left) in east Co. Cork is the centre of Irish gastronomic excellence. A delightful town in its own right, it has more fine restaurants than any other place of comparable size in Ireland. Garinish Island, just a short boat ride from the coast at Glengarriff, contains one of the most remarkable gardens in Ireland (left), an exotic mixture of the classical and the tropical. Of all of the monuments in Cork or elsewhere, perhaps none has passed so completely into the language as Blarney Castle (above), a stronghold of the McCarthys which contains the famous stone which, if kissed, is said to convey the promise of permanent eloquence.

In the south-west corner of the country, the 'Kingdom' of Kerry is a special place. It draws more visitors to its astonishingly varied sights than any other county in the country. The mild Atlantic climate produces wonderful summer flora as in the fuchsia hedge (opposite) which stands behind the old-style and wonderfully plural finger posts. Kerry would be famous for Killarney alone, the single most visited tourist site in the country. Lough Leane (above) is the largest of the Killarney lakes with the high peaks of the MacGillycuddy Reeks rising above it. On its shores stands Ross Castle (below), a former fortress of the O'Donoghues.

The forbidding Great Skellig Island off the coast of Kerry contains monastic ruins (left). Dunmore Head (right) at the end of the Dingle Peninsula, is the most westerly point in Europe. The Dingle Peninsula has many beehive huts like the one below and there are still traditional thatched cottages (below left).

Sneem exhibition park houses a collection of statues and sculptures (below right).

On the Great Skellig (above left).
In Dingle Town (left).
Muckross House, Killarney (top), the former home of the Herbert family, dates from 1843.
Gallarus Oratory (above) on the Dingle Peninsula is a perfectly preserved corbelled oratory. It is built entirely of dry stone with no mortar. It has stood here, surviving all winds and weather, for over 1,000 years.

Limerick city and county lies to the west of the Golden Vale and south of the Shannon Estuary. Castlematrix (above) was a stronghold of the Earls of Desmond. The ninth earl was murdered here by his servants in 1487. The pretty village of Adare (opposite top) is celebrated for its beautifully maintained thatched cottages. King John's Castle (opposite middle) beside the Shannon in Limerick city is one of the earliest and most formidable of all Norman fortifications in Ireland. Glin Castle (right) overlooks the pleasant shores of the Shannon Estuary.

Co. Tipperary was dominated by the Butlers in the east and the Fitzgeralds in the west. The great Butler castle of Cahir (above right) is one of the best restored medieval fortified houses in Ireland. But these rich Tipperary plains – the Golden Vale is mostly in this county – was home to much earlier and more ancient rulers. The great royal-ecclesiastical site on the Rock of Cashel (above) dominates all the flat countryside around. Originally the seat of the Gaelic kings of Munster, it developed into an important ecclesiastical centre in early Christian times and contains – in Cormac's chapel – one of the earliest examples of Romanesque architecture in Ireland. Holycross Abbey (right), a beautifully restored Cistercian foundation, stands on the banks of the River Suir a few kilometres south of Thurles.

Co. Clare is bounded by Galway Bay to the north, the Shannon and its lakes to its east, the Shannon Estuary to the south and the Atlantic Ocean to the west. Although part of the province of Munster, it feels more like an extension of Connacht – and indeed some old maps show it as part of Connacht. The Poulnabrone Dolmen (above) marks the burial site of a late Stone-Age farming community. It has stood here for almost 6,000 years. Killaloe Cathedral (below), at the southern end of Lough Derg, occupies an ancient Christian site. The cathedral itself dates to the late twelfth century. The massive bulk of Bunratty Castle (right) was originally built as an early Norman fortification in the thirteenth century. However, this present structure dates from the fifteenth century when it was rebuilt by the MacConmaras. It later became an O'Brien stronghold.

O'Brien's Tower (left) at the Cliffs of Moher at sunset. The little spa town of Lisdoonvarna (above) has been a popular resort since the nineteenth century. It owes its original popularity to its spring waters and their curative properties. It is now the location of one of Ireland's leading bachelor festivals, in which men from far and wide come in search of wives. It is also an important traditional music centre. The Craggaunowen project (below) is based at Quin, Co. Clare. The photograph shows a replica crannóg, a reed and thatched lake dwelling of a sort that was typical of this region in early medieval times.

'o. Galway and the Aran Islands in Galway Bay are a microcosm of what we mean by the phrase 'the *Vest of Ireland'. The great Stone-Age fort of Dun Aenghus (above left) on Inismór comprises three *oncentric rows of stone defences forming a semi-circle on the landward side, with a sheer drop into the *tlantic Ocean at the cliff-face. This astonishing work is one of the most dramatic antiquities in the *hole country. The ruined cathedral and the round tower at Kilmacduagh (left) stands at the site of a *eventh-century monastery founded by St Colman. The round tower leans slightly off the vertical *lthough not as dramatically as the Tower of Pisa. The great stone tower house at Aughanure (above) *as built by the O'Flahertys around 1500. The O'Flahertys controlled much of the countryside *urrounding Galway city and were a constant threat to its civic order.*

Lynch's Castle in Galway (left), now a bank, stands at the junction of Shop Street and Upper Abbeygate Street. The original structure dates from the early sixteenth century and the exterior walls still bear the arms of King Henry VII, the English monarch who reigned from 1485 to 1509. Galway has been fortunate in its urban renewal in recent decades and its well-maintained narrow streets (below left) draw many visitors in the summer. The Spanish Arch (above) is a reminder of the centuries-long trading links between Spain and the West of Ireland, while the summer street scene (below) could almost be in Spain itself.

Clifden Castle (left) was the house of John Darcy, the founder of the nearby town of Clifden. It dates from the early nineteenth century. Kylemore Abbey (above) was originally built by a wealthy Englishman but is now a boarding school run by the Benedictine nuns.

Clifden (above and left) is the capital of Connemara, standing at the head of Clifden Bay and framed by the Twelve Bens on the landward side. Montalto House, near Ballynahinch (above left), stands in the heart of Connemara.

On the north Mayo coast the Ceide Fields (left) is a 12 square kilometre field system, dating from the Stone Age, which has been excavated in recent years. The fields with their stone wall enclosures have been preserved intact by the blanket bog that covered them. This brilliant archaeological achievement has revealed one of the most ancient habitations in Europe. The attractive town of Westport (below) was developed as an estate town in the shadow of Westport House. The current house, whose entrance is shown above, dates from the eighteenth century but many of the great families of Mayo – the O'Malleys, the Bourkes and the Brownes – have lived on this site.

Westport House (opposite top) is the finest classical country house in Co. Mayo. The town of Killala (opposite middle), at the head of the Bay of the same name, was occupied for a time by French revolutionary troops under General Humbert in 1798. Humbert's actual landing place was at nearby Kilcummin (left). The National Famine Monument (above) stands just outside Westport in the dramatic shadow of Croagh Patrick.

Co. Fermanagh is dominated by Upper and Lower Lough Erne, the waterways that have traditionally provided a natural line of defence for south-west Ulster. The town of Enniskillen (above right) is built on an island site. It was a stronghold of the Maguire clan in Gaelic times and was equally important in the early seventeenth century in defending the new plantation of Ulster. Both Upper and Lower Lough Erne contain many islands, of which Boa Island with its Janus-faced stone carvings (above), is one of the most famous. Devenish Island (right) is an important early Christian site. This photograph shows the round tower on Devenish, one of the last to be built in Ireland.

The late medieval cross in the cemetery on Devenish (above).
Two kinds of Co. Fermanagh house. The thatched red-washed house (above right) was originally built as an eighteenth-century farmhouse. It possesses the symmetry and good proportions typical of that era. Florence Court (right) is simply one of the finest big houses in Ireland. Although very grand, it too displays the symmetry, tact and order typical of classical architecture. Florence Court was built for the earls of Enniskillen in the 1760s.

Sligo is a county that will forever be associated with the life and work of W.B. Yeats, who is buried here in Drumcliff cemetery, 'under bare Ben Bulben's head' (above, Slidefile). His most quoted poem was 'The Lake Isle of Innisfree', pictured above left, while he also wrote of Lissadell House (far left): 'The light of evening, Lissadell/ Great windows open to the south. / Two girls in silk kimonos, both/ Beautiful, one a gazelle.' Yeats's mother's family, the Pollexfens, were merchants and traders in Sligo (left). The town is the venue for the annual Yeats Summer School, one of the oldest and most prestigious schools in Ireland.

Two important ancient burial sites in Co. Sligo. Knocknarea (top) has a great mound of stones on its summit, said to mark the spot where the legendary Queen Maeve of Connacht is buried. In the foreground stand some stones from a satellite tomb. The stone cairn at Heapstown (above), near Lough Arrow, is believed to contain a passage grave which has yet to be excavated.
Donegal is the most northerly county in Ireland, even though it is not part of Northern Ireland! Donegal town, with its castle (right), traditionally guarded the south-western approaches to this land of wild and rugged scenery. The ruins of the old Franciscan friary also in the town (above right) mark a connection between the Franciscan order and the local O'Donnell chieftains that lasted until the collapse of the Gaelic world in 1600.

Donegal contrasts. Doone Lake near Portnoo (above left) and a rick of turf standing in the shadow of Mount Errigal, the highest mountain in the county (left). The Castle of Glenveagh (above) stands at the centre of one of Ireland's greatest national parks.

The Grianan of Aileach (above left) is an ancient stone fort, probably dating from the fifth century, commanding a wonderful view over Lough Foyle and Lough Swilly. This great fortification was a stronghold of the O'Neill dynasty who dominated much of Gaelic Ulster. The isolated and beautiful settlement of Glencolmcille (left) on the northern shores of Donegal Bay, is typical of many such coastal settlements in the county. The Marian Shrine at the Gap of Manore (above) overlooks magnificent countryside typical of Co. Donegal.

At the far north-western end of Co. Donegal the landscape around Bloody Foreland is truly magnificent.

Derry is the principal city of the north-west and its main thoroughfare is Shipquay Street (above, Slidefile). At Downhill, near Limavady, Co. Derry, the eccentric eighteenth-century bishop of Derry, Frederick Hervey, built a palace, some of the outbuildings of which are shown below.

The entrance to St Columb's Cathedral in Derry, showing the city arms (above). The Mussenden Temple (opposite top) at Downhill and the ruins of Hervey's palace (opposite middle) stand on the north Derry coast. The fine panoramic view of Derry city (right) is taken from the east bank of the Foyle: it shows the historic walled city with St Columb's at its centre.

Co. Tyrone lies in the centre of Ulster and has many historical associations. The Sperrin Mountains country (above) dominates much of the county. There is a long tradition of emigration from this part of Ireland to the United States. The plaque (above right) commemorates the ancestral home of Ulysses S. Grant, victorious general in the US Civil War and president of the United States. The Ulster History Park (right), an open-air museum of human settlement, is situated near Omagh, the county town.

Armagh is one of the finest classical towns in Ireland. The Mall (above) is its centrepiece. The squat Church of Ireland Cathedral of St Patrick (above right) marks the site of a very early Christian shrine. The library (right) is a fine, restrained public building.

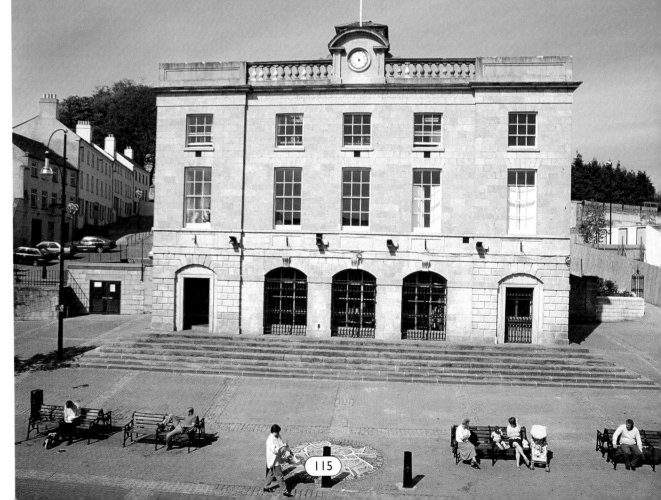

The Palace Stables in Armagh (above) and the Armagh Planetarium (right).

The Diamond in Monaghan Town (above) and the broad main street of Carrickmacross (below).

The Ulster Folk and Transport Museum at Cultra, Co. Down, just outside Belfast, has the most important and comprehensive collection of its kind in Ireland, north or south. The Folk Park (above left), with reconstructions of traditional villages, streets and housing types, is especially impressive. The Tomb of St Patrick (left) in the church at Downpatrick marks the spot where the saint is believed to lie. Above is the pretty town of Warrenpoint in south Co. Down, with the Mourne Mountains in the background.

Co. Down ranges from the wealthy hinterland of Belfast in the north and east to the rugged upland country of the south. Bangor (left) is the principal town in north Co. Down. The great classical house of Castle Ward on the shores of Strangford Lough (above) was built in the 1760s for Benjamin Ward, first Viscount Bangor. Silent Valley (below) is typical of the upland Mourne country in the south of the county near the border with the Republic.

Belfast City Hall (above) is a symbol of the city's Edwardian swagger. There are beautiful grounds at Stormont Park (above right) with the parliament buildings in the background, and the Botanic Gardens boasts this superb tropical glasshouse (right).

Queen's University Belfast (above left) was founded in 1845 and is the principal university in Northern Ireland. Co. Antrim on the north-eastern corner of the island has a wide variety of scenery and artefacts. Here is a view along the north Antrim coast at White Park Bay (left). The pretty village of Glenarm (above) stands between the glen of the same name and its shallow, curving bay.

The beautiful Glenariff Forest Park (above) is one of Co. Antrim's many wonderful views. Dunluce Castle (above right), sited on a clifftop on the north Antrim coast, was a stronghold of the McDonnells until it collapsed into the sea in 1639. The Glens of Antrim (right) are justly famous: there are nine in all, running from the central plateau towards the coast.